CONTENTS

All <u>underlined</u> words are explained in the glossary on page 60

FRONT COVER IWM SITE BELF 000599
LEFT Flags flying on HMS *Belfast*, C35 – Pendant Number (left), Golf Golf Charlie November – Radio Call Sign (right) IWM SITE BELF 318

WELCOME ON BOARD

WELCOME TO HMS BELFAST, one of the branches of IWM (Imperial War Museums) and a unique reminder of Britain's naval heritage. Moored in the Pool of London, the *Belfast* plays an important part in helping IWM fulfil our remit, ensuring that present and future generations understand the causes and, most importantly, the consequences of conflict. Originally founded in 1917, IWM chronicles the impact of war during the twentieth and twenty-first centuries at all levels and includes records of the experiences of men and women in the forces as well as civilians, all of whom have been caught up in conflict over the past century. IWM continues to collect today and thus exists as a record not only of our past but of ongoing conflict and its effect on our society and daily lives.

IWM consists of five branches, three of which are in London: HMS *Belfast*, our largest accessioned object; Churchill War Rooms, housed in the underground complex in Whitehall where Winston Churchill and his Cabinet met throughout the Second World War; and IWM London in Lambeth, which is closed until July 2013 as part of our ambitious redevelopment project, Transforming IWM London. This branch will partially re-open in July 2013 with a new family exhibition – *Horrible Histories*®: *Spies* – and a new programme of art and photography displays as well as some of our permanent galleries. In summer 2014 IWM London will fully re-open as we launch our brand new galleries to mark the centenary of the start of the First World War. We will also unveil our transformed atrium, new shops and a park-side café.

Outside London, we are fortunate to have IWM Duxford, near Cambridge, considered to be Europe's premier aviation museum. The site incorporates buildings dating from the First and Second World Wars, when the airfield was active, and is also the home of the American Air Museum. Our fifth and newest branch is IWM North in Manchester, housed in a building designed by Daniel Libeskind representing the world torn apart by conflict.

The public can also access our extensive photographic, film, sound, documents and printed books collections for private research. For more information on access and the wide-ranging and varied programme of exhibitions, events and educational sessions at all five branches, please visit **iwm.org.uk**.

Finally, I would like to emphasise that we rely greatly on support of all kinds: from IWM Friends and our amazing teams of volunteers, through to those people who support us with donations and legacies. If you would like to help us, please visit our website for further details.

Thank you, and please visit us again soon.

Diane Lees, Director-General
IWM

HMS BELFAST IS A LANDMARK. Alongside its neighbours, the Tower of London and Tower Bridge, it is an essential part of the London skyline. It marks the third of three major chapters in London's history, from medieval times, through the Victorian industrial and technological revolution, to the major role played by Britain in the struggle to resist Nazi efforts to dominate the world. No ship surviving in Britain today has witnessed historic events of the magnitude that *Belfast* has – having taken part in one of the greatest naval engagements of the Second World War in the sinking of the *Scharnhorst*; surviving Arctic conditions to bring relief to Britain's ally, Russia, in 1943; leading the way on D-Day, 6 June 1944; and playing a major role in Britain's support for the United Nations forces fighting in Korea from 1950 to 1952.

In each of these episodes the ship was not merely a fighting machine, but the home of many thousands of sailors. It is these brave men and women who gave up their livings and even their lives to defend freedom and the right to life of others, not just in Britain, but all over the world. Conditions on board were never the stuff of luxury. Often, when crowding her lower decks with survivors of sinkings, attacks and evacuations – such as that of internees from China in 1945 – *Belfast's* sailors gave up any semblance of comfort for the good of those who had suffered and survived far worse deprivations than themselves.

What these emergency guests – and today's visitors – would encounter was not a scene of confusion, of discontent at their lot, or even discomfort; but a world in which a crew worked together, making sacrifices for their fellow sailors, and also enjoying a sense of community. These were men with families, friends and loved ones from whom they would be separated and out of touch for months on end. The *Belfast*, with facilities from barbering to bathrooms, from messing to mass, and from doctors to dentists, was a place where the crew worked hard and played hard. This was their home. This was their community.

And it was a community that lived on way past any period of a sailor's service. Today we still welcome back members of the HMS *Belfast* Association to relive and pass on to younger generations – who happily have no experience of war – their recollections and the stories of their lives afloat. To the incredulous young – curious to know as much how toilet practices were observed, as how people can possibly function in arctic ice and under constant fire – the ship, its preserved scenes, and its endless ladders between decks and the bowels of its massive structure, provides a living answer to their questions and allows them a unique insight into life afloat.

Today the ship boasts a thriving Learning Department. She is kept ship-shape by a team of conservators – many of them unpaid volunteers. And she is financially supported by visitors and the generosity of those conscious of our debt to that generation. I hope you have enjoyed your visit. I hope it has helped you to better understand the importance of the contribution of a generation that gave so much to enable us to enjoy freedom, peace and prosperity. And I hope too that you will make your own contribution to ensure that this historic vessel is forever preserved, and its work is allowed to continue for generations to come.

Phil Reed, Director,
HMS *Belfast*

PLAN OF THE SHIP

Your tour: ⟶ follow the route to explore the ship

① Audio guide points: tune in as you tour HMS *Belfast*

1	Introduction
2	Quarterdeck
3	Gun Turret Experience ('Y' Turret)
4	Torpedo Flat
5	Laundry
6	Mailroom
7	Chapel
8	Sound Reproduction Room
9	Boiler Room
10	Engine Room
11	Butcher and Potato Store
12	Baker and 1950s Mess Deck
13	Galley
14	Sick Bay, Dispensary and Dentist
15	Gyro Compass and Forward Steering Position
16	NAAFI
17	Provision Issue Room (Rum Ration)
18	Arctic Messdeck
19	Punishment Cells
20	'B' Turret 6-inch Shell Room and Magazine
21	Fo'c'sle
22	Admiral's Bridge
23	Bridge Wireless Office and Electronic Warfare Office
24	Gun Direction Platform
25	Compass Platform
26	Operations Room
27	Admiral's and Captain's Sea Cabins
28	VHF Room
29	Boat Deck
30	4-inch HA/LA Guns

Life on board: Main exhibition decks

How it works: Below decks

Where it all happens: Upper decks

♿ **Access:** For assistance please contact a member of staff on arrival.

⚠ **Safety:** HMS *Belfast* is a warship designed for active service at sea. Please take great care as you tour the ship, especially on the stairs. Look out for overhead and floor level hazards. Areas may be closed for conservation.

☕ **Café**

🍸 **Upper Deck bar:** Opens Easter 2013

☀ **Viewpoints**

🌐 **Shop**

⇅ **Lift**

🚻 **Toilets**

ⓘ **Conservation and Information Centre**

ⓔ **Exhibition Galleries**

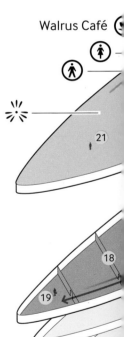

Walrus Café

PREVIOUS PAGE HMS *Belfast* moored in the Pool of London IWM SITE BELF 602

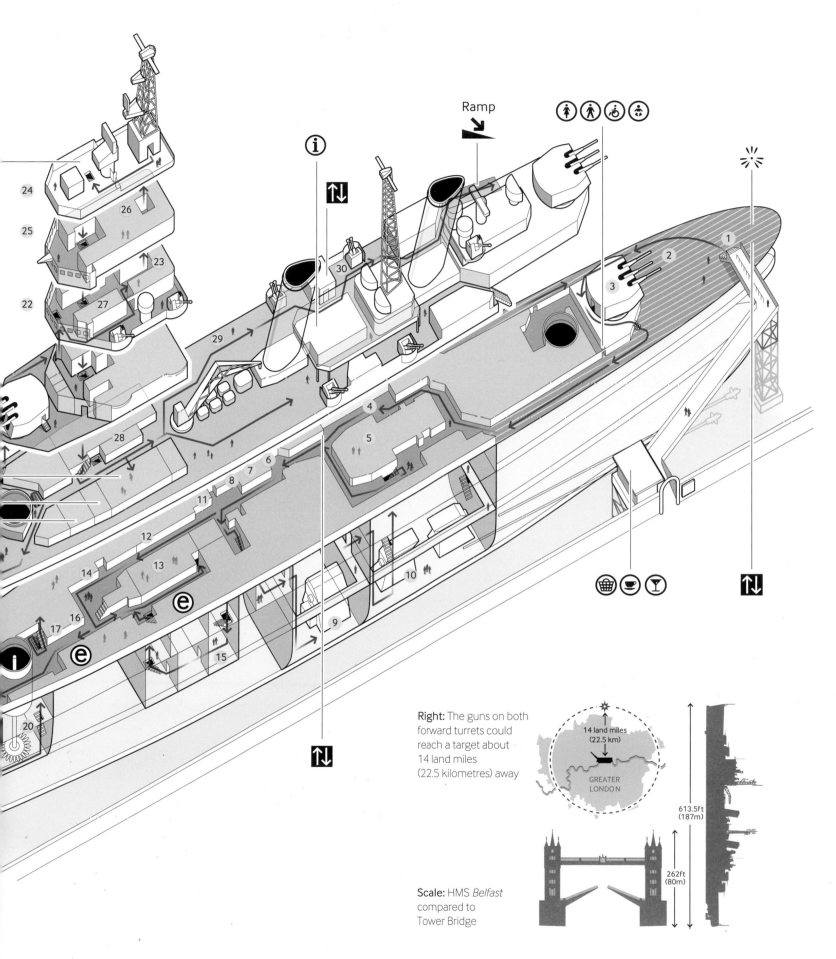

Ramp

24
25
22
26
23
27
28
29
30

1
2
3
4
5
6
7
8
11
12
13
14
16
17
20
9
10
15

Right: The guns on both forward turrets could reach a target about 14 land miles (22.5 kilometres) away

14 land miles (22.5 km)

GREATER LONDON

613.5ft (187m)

262ft (80m)

Scale: HMS *Belfast* compared to Tower Bridge

THE LIFE STORY OF HMS BELFAST

'WE WERE ABOUT TO EMBARK ON THE BIGGEST MILITARY OPERATION THE WORLD HAD EVER KNOWN.'

Engineer-Lieutenant Charles Simpson on D-Day

ORIGINS

THE TERM 'CRUISER' dates back to the days of sailing ships, when large <u>frigates</u> could be deployed to operate independently against enemy commerce raiders and merchant ships. During the nineteenth century, when sail gave way to steam and wooden ships were replaced by vessels built of iron, and later of steel, the cruiser evolved into a powerful warship which was used to patrol the British Empire's far-flung maritime trade routes.

Both before and during the First World War (1914–1918), cruisers were increasingly required to undertake a wide variety of tasks, ranging from their traditional role of commerce protection to direct support of the Navy's battleships. In the aftermath of the Washington Naval Treaty of 1922, which imposed restrictions upon the size and armament of all types of warship, British cruiser construction began to produce two distinct types of vessel: 'heavy cruisers' with 8-inch guns and <u>displacements</u> of up to 10,000 tons, whose size and great fuel capacity made them particularly suitable for long-range deployment in defence of trade, and smaller 'light cruisers' with 6-inch guns for more offensive deployment in support of the battle fleet.

In the mid 1930s, however, a new type of vessel emerged which combined the size advantage of the earlier generation of heavy cruisers with large numbers of rapid-firing 6-inch guns. These large light cruisers were built in great numbers, and many of them continued in service long after the end of the Second World War.

PREVIOUS PAGES HMS *Belfast's* silver bell, presented by the people of Belfast in October 1948. IWM SITE BELF 287; Improvised 'helicopter transfer bag' used to deliver mail, 1960s IWM SITE BELF 385 **BELOW** HMS *Belfast* at full speed on the measured mile range off Greenock on 23 May 1939. The 4-inch secondary battery mountings and main armament Director Control Towers have not yet been fitted. IWM HU 43767

LEFT Tread plate fixed to the deck near the gangway. Red appears on the port side, and the starboard side uses green. IWM SITE BELF 329
BELOW Champagne bottle ribbon from HMS *Belfast*'s launch on 17 March 1938 IWM SITE BELF 384

DESIGN AND CONSTRUCTION

IN 1936 the Admiralty decided to order two enlarged and improved versions of the large light cruisers of the 'Southampton' class with sixteen 6-inch guns in four quadruple turrets, on a displacement of 10,000 tons – the maximum permitted under the terms of the Washington Treaty. The two ships were called *Edinburgh* and *Belfast*, which followed the policy of naming the 'Southamptons' after British towns and cities.

In the event, it proved impossible to manufacture effective quadruple 6-inch mountings due to ballistic problems with the ammunition, and the final design specified an improved version of the successful triple mounts used in the 'Southampton' class. Here the middle gun is set back to stop the blast wave from the other shells interfering with the **trajectory** of its shell as it left the muzzle just behind the two outer barrels. The weight saved was used to improve armour protection and to increase the ships' anti-aircraft armament by 50 per cent.

Construction of the second ship of the *Edinburgh* class was assigned by tender to Messrs Harland & Wolff of Belfast on 21 September 1936, and the vessel was launched by Anne Chamberlain, wife of the Prime Minister, on St Patrick's Day, 17 March 1938.

After fitting out and builder's trials, HMS *Belfast* was commissioned into the Royal Navy on 5 August 1939 under the command of Captain G A Scott DSO RN.

THE NAVY ESTIMATES FOR THAT YEAR SHOW THAT BELFAST'S COST WAS £2,141,514, INCLUDING £75,000 FOR THE GUNS AND £66,500 FOR AIRCRAFT

EARLY WAR SERVICE

ON THE OUTBREAK OF WAR WITH GERMANY in September 1939, HMS *Belfast* formed part of the 18th Cruiser Squadron operating out of the Home Fleet's main base at Scapa Flow in Orkney.

Over the course of the next few weeks, the ship was constantly on patrol in northern waters as part of the Royal Navy's efforts to impose a maritime blockade on Germany. This work entailed stopping and searching merchant ships to prevent German civilians or 'contraband' – war supplies – getting to Germany. On 9 October, HMS *Belfast* successfully intercepted the German liner SS *Cap Norte*, which was trying to return to Germany disguised as a neutral vessel, the Swedish ship *Ancona*. *Cap Norte* had sailed from Argentina carrying many German armed forces reservists trying to get home to rejoin their units. The liner was boarded and sent under armed guard to a British port. The first officer of *Cap Norte* was furious, as he had been captured in similar circumstances as a young officer in August 1914. *Cap Norte* was the largest enemy merchant ship intercepted to date, and under Admiralty law *Belfast*'s crew received 'prize money' in the form of a cash gratuity for her capture.

BELOW LEFT Cap ribbon belonging to one of the crew of the SS *Cap Norte* IWM SITE BELF 389
BOTTOM The German liner SS *Cap Norte* of the Hamburg Süd-American line, captured by HMS *Belfast* on 9 October 1939 IWM HU 10272
RIGHT Hilt of a bayonet belonging to one of the crew of the SS *Cap Norte* IWM SITE BELF 390

'SUDDENLY THERE WAS A TERRIFIC THUD, AND THEN THERE WAS DEAD SILENCE AND THEN
A SHAKING UP AND DOWN, AS IF YOU WERE SHAKING A DOLL UP AND DOWN.
THAT WAS THE POWER OF A MAGNETIC MINE.'

Ordnance Artificer John Harrison

MINED!

THE JUBILATION OF THE EARLY SUCCESS in seizing *Cap Norte* was short-lived. Shortly before 11am on 21 November 1939, whilst leaving the Firth of Forth for a gunnery exercise, HMS *Belfast* was rocked by the violent detonation of a magnetic mine.

Although casualties were mercifully light, the ship's back was broken, and the damage to her hull and machinery caused by the whiplash effect of the explosion was so severe that it was thought she would have to be scrapped. However, naval architects became convinced that she could be repaired, and almost three years were to elapse before she could be made fit for action.

ABOVE A photograph taken in Devonport Dockyard in 1940 showing the mine damage to *Belfast*'s hull IWM MH 23670
TOP HMS *Belfast* shortly after her mining in the Firth of Forth. Members of the ship's company can just be seen getting ready to launch life rafts from the Quarterdeck. IWM HU 16012

ARCTIC CONVOYS

WHEN SHE FINALLY REJOINED THE HOME FLEET in November 1942, under the command of Captain (later Admiral Sir Frederick) Parham, HMS *Belfast* was the largest and arguably the most powerful cruiser in the Royal Navy. Not only had she been 'bulged' amidships, increasing her standard displacement to 11,500 tons and significantly improving her stability, but she had also been equipped with the most up-to-date <u>radar</u> and fire control systems. She was soon in action in one of the most dangerous theatres of the naval war as flagship of the 10th Cruiser Squadron, responsible for providing close-range heavy cover for the Arctic convoys taking supplies to the Soviet Union.

Wearing the flag of Rear-Admiral (later Vice-Admiral Sir Robert) Burnett, HMS *Belfast* left Iceland on 21 February 1943 for the Russian port of Murmansk in support of convoy JW53.

Although the Germans failed to prevent the convoy from reaching its destination, gale force winds caused severe damage to the warships and merchant vessels alike.

Apart from occasional offensive sweeps with the battleships and aircraft carriers of the Home Fleet, HMS *Belfast* was to spend most of 1943 in the icy waters of the Arctic.

'WE WENT ROUND TO THE ARCTIC...OUR DUTY STATION WAS THE DENMARK STRAITS, BACKWARDS AND FORWARDS, MAKING SURE NO GERMAN SHIPS GOT OUT. ONE EARLY MORNING I WANTED TO GET TO "A" TURRET ON THE UPPER DECK. WAITING FOR THE BIG ONES TO COME OVER, I DASHED, GOT MY HAND ON THE TURRET DOOR AND A BIG ONE CAME OVER, SWEPT ME FROM MY FEET, BUT I DIDN'T GET WASHED OVERBOARD BECAUSE MY HAND WAS FROZEN ON THE TURRET HANDLE.'

Ordnance Artificer John Harrison

LEFT Sailors and Royal Marines pose for the camera during a break from the essential task of clearing ice from HMS *Belfast*'s upper decks. Apart from rendering guns and fire control systems inoperable, an accumulation of ice could make the ship top-heavy and seriously affect her stability in the event of damage. IWM HU 8799 **BELOW LEFT** HMS *Belfast* leaving Iceland on 21 February 1943 to escort convoy JW53 on its voyage to Russia IWM A 15530 **BELOW RIGHT** View from the open bridge of HMS *Sheffield*, one of HMS *Belfast*'s half-sisters, as she fights her way through heavy seas on convoy duty in the North Atlantic in 1943 IWM A 14890

THE BATTLE OF NORTH CAPE

BETWEEN THE BEGINNING OF NOVEMBER AND THE MIDDLE OF DECEMBER 1943, no less than three eastbound and two westbound Arctic convoys reached their destinations without loss, and the commander-in-chief of the German Navy, Grand Admiral Doenitz, came under increasing pressure to sanction a <u>sortie</u> by one of Germany's few remaining heavy surface ships to interrupt the flow of supplies via the Arctic convoy route. On the evening of 25 December, the battle cruiser *Scharnhorst*, her messdecks adorned with traditional Christmas decorations, set sail from Langefjord with five <u>destroyers</u>. Her mission: to attack and destroy convoys JW55B and RA55A as they passed the northern tip of Norway.

Unknown to the Germans, British Intelligence was intercepting and deciphering German signals, and within hours the Admiralty had informed Commander-in-Chief, Home Fleet Admiral Bruce Fraser that *Scharnhorst* was at sea, giving him plenty of time to organise his forces. Rear-Admiral Burnett in HMS *Belfast*, along with the cruisers *Norfolk* and *Sheffield*, screened the convoys and kept *Scharnhorst* in action. Meanwhile, Admiral Fraser in the battleship HMS *Duke of York*, accompanied by the cruiser HMS *Jamaica* and four destroyers, cut her off from the south.

EARLY IN THE MORNING OF 26 DECEMBER, the *Scharnhorst*, having sent her destroyer escorts back to base due to extreme weather conditions, encountered Burnett and his cruisers only to be driven off after being hit by one of HMS *Norfolk*'s 8-inch shells. After a further unsuccessful attempt to break through to the convoys, the *Scharnhorst* retreated at high speed with *Belfast* and *Sheffield* in hot pursuit, driving the enemy towards Admiral Fraser and the 14-inch guns of HMS *Duke of York*. Shortly after gaining radar contact, the *Duke of York* succeeded in hitting the German battle cruiser with her first <u>salvo</u>.

Although *Scharnhorst* twisted and turned, she was unable to shake off her tormentors, and eventually her fire slackened sufficiently to allow Admiral Fraser to send in his destroyers. Hit by at least three torpedoes and pounded by heavy guns at point-blank range, the battle cruiser was now dead in the water. Finally, the *Belfast* and *Jamaica* were ordered to sink her with torpedoes. Even as HMS *Belfast* fired, *Scharnhorst*'s radar blip vanished, to be followed by a series of muffled underwater explosions as she slipped beneath the waves. Only 36 out of her complement of 1,963 men were picked up by the British. The extreme cold meant that the German sailors could not have survived more than a few minutes in the icy water.

'WHEN [SCHARNHORST] WAS ACTUALLY SUNK, A SMELL CAME DOWN THE VENTILATION TRUNKING OF FUEL OIL, ONE OF THE FOULEST SMELLS IN ALL THE WORLD. I THOUGHT, "POOR DEVILS". SWIMMING IN THAT, CAN YOU IMAGINE?'

Engineer-Lieutenant Charles Simpson, who was in the engine room for the Battle of North Cape

RIGHT *Scharnhorst* shell splinter IWM SITE BELF 387

TOP HMS *Duke of York* opens fire. The much greater weight of the British battleship's 14-inch shells gave her a significant advantage over *Scharnhorst* in a gunnery duel, especially when firing at long range IWM A 7550 **ABOVE LEFT** The torpedomen of HMS *Jamaica* who finally dispatched the *Scharnhorst* IWM A 21167 **ABOVE RIGHT** Originally intended as lightly armoured 'pocket battleships', *Scharnhorst* and her sister ship *Gneisenau* were redesigned on Hitler's orders with heavy protective armour and a very high top speed of 33 knots (61 km/h). *Scharnhorst*'s main armament of nine 28 cm (11 in.) guns was, however, smaller than that normally mounted in a battleship, and she was always described by the Royal Navy as a battle cruiser. Able to outrun any existing battleship and out fight any cruiser, she was ideally suited for commerce raiding. IWM HU 1042

OPERATION 'TUNGSTEN'

ON 30 MARCH 1944, HMS *Belfast* sailed from Scapa Flow in company with a powerful force of battleships and aircraft carriers. Their objective was the *Tirpitz*, Germany's last surviving heavy battleship, moored in the supposedly impregnable anchorage of Altenfjord in northern Norway.

In the early hours of 3 April, having approached within 120 miles of the Norwegian coast, the carriers launched 42 bombers and 80 fighters in the largest air strike yet undertaken by the Fleet Air Arm. *Tirpitz* was hit by 15 bombs and although not sunk, was incapable of putting to sea for several months. She was finally destroyed by heavy bombers from 617 Squadron RAF in November 1944.

BOTTOM Barracuda bombers from the fleet carriers *Victorious* and *Furious* flying over Altenfjord during the course of Operation 'Tungsten' IWM A 22631
BELOW LEFT The battleship *Tirpitz*, a solitary, brooding shape amidst the wintry landscape of one of her Norwegian lairs. With a main armament of eight 38 cm (15 in.) guns, *Tirpitz* was one of the most powerful ships in European waters. IWM HU 50947 **BELOW RIGHT** 'Bombing-up' a Barracuda prior to the attack on *Tirpitz* on 3 April 1944 IWM 22640

D-DAY BOMBARDMENT

EVER SINCE THE DISASTROUS DIEPPE RAID IN 1942, when the assaulting troops had been cut down by well-protected German gun positions, Allied amphibious operations had been supported by heavy naval bombardments. Now, for D-Day, the Allied invasion of Normandy on 6 June 1944, the bombardment force comprised 5 battleships, 2 monitors, 20 cruisers and 65 destroyers. But this was only a part of the total force of 2,700 seagoing vessels and 1,900 smaller craft which were deployed in support of Operation 'Neptune', the naval side of the Normandy landings.

This huge armada was divided into two naval task forces and five assault forces, one for each of the main landing beaches. Each of the assault forces was in turn supported by its own naval bombardment force. As flagship of Bombardment Force E, HMS *Belfast* was part of the Eastern Naval Task Force, with responsibility for supporting the British and Canadian assaults on 'Gold' and 'Juno' beaches.

One of the crew, Brian Butler, remembered with pride that 'we were right at the head of the convoy...we went in right behind the minesweepers'. In the early hours of the morning, *Belfast* went to action stations.

'AT 4AM WE WENT TO ACTION STATIONS, AND ALREADY COULD SEE THE GLOW OF RED FIRES BEING STARTED BY OUR BOMBERS, AND THE STREAMS OF RED TRACERS BEING SENT UP BY THE ENEMY'S ACK ACK [ANTI-AIRCRAFT FIRE].' Lieutenant Peter Brooke-Smith

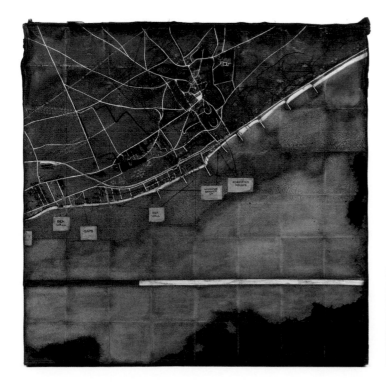

LEFT Section of D-Day briefing model showing German defences IWM SITE BELF 394 **BELOW** Rear-Admiral Dalrymple-Hamilton, commanding Bombardment Force E, on the bridge of HMS *Belfast* with Captain Parham (smoking a pipe) in the early hours of 6 June 1944 IWM HU 65372

Many *Belfast* veterans believe that their ship was the first to open fire on 6 June. However, this does not seem to have been the case, although more by accident than design. As Peter Brooke-Smith wrote:

'WE WERE FURIOUSLY INDIGNANT WHEN AT 0523 A CRUISER TO THE WESTWARD OF US, PROBABLY HMS ORION, OPENED FIRE AND THUS FORESTALLED US THE HONOUR OF BEING THE FIRST SHIP TO FIRE A SHOT IN THE SECOND FRONT. WE NEED NOT HAVE WORRIED: REX NORTH, SUNDAY PICTORIAL'S WAR CORRESPONDENT WHO WE HAD ONBOARD, UNBLUSHINGLY GAVE US THAT HONOUR.'

Belfast's log records that she opened fire three minutes later, at 0527, 'with full **broadside** to port'.

This first target was a German battery in the village of La Marefontaine. As a result of *Belfast*'s bombardment, the battery played no meaningful role in the defence of the beaches. The badly demoralised garrison from the 1716th Artillery Regiment was subsequently attacked by fighter bombers, encircled by tanks and destroyed by the 7th Battalion, the Green Howards. *Belfast* was one of the larger warships, with a fully equipped sick bay, a surgeon-commander and two surgeon-lieutenants. As the day wore on, a trickle of casualties began to arrive on board, the first few by motor launch at 1300.

Also on board HMS *Belfast* was the famous Hollywood film director George Stephens, officially present to record the D-Day landings for the United States Signals Corps.

Stephens had also brought along a 16mm hand-held camera for his own use. The resulting footage is the only known colour film of *Belfast* taken during the Second World War.

Over the course of the next five weeks, *Belfast* was almost continuously in action, firing thousands of rounds from her batteries in support of Allied troops fighting their way inland against skilful and determined German opposition. Her last shoot took place in company with the battleship HMS *Rodney* and the monitor HMS *Roberts* on 8 July 1945 during the course of heavy fighting for the city of Caen. Two days later, the battle lines having moved beyond the **range** of her 6-inch guns, HMS *Belfast* set sail for Plymouth Devonport and a well-earned refit prior to being despatched to the Far East. She had fired her guns in anger for the last time in European waters.

ABOVE HMS *Belfast* using her 4-inch secondary battery against German shore positions in Normandy on the night of 27 June 1944 IWM A 24325
RIGHT (TOP TO BOTTOM) Stills from film taken on D-Day showing HMS *Belfast* bombarding the coast. Note the landing craft, heading towards the beach.
IWM FLM 4017, IWM FLM 4015, IWM FLM 4016

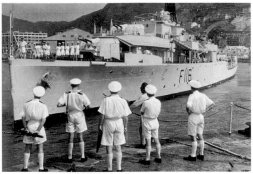

LEFT Children of British and Commonwealth civilian internees are entertained at a party held on board HMS *Belfast* in Shanghai on 28 September 1945 IWM A 30854
ABOVE HMS *Amethyst* pictured in Hong Kong harbour following repairs to the damage inflicted by Chinese Communist artillery in the Yangtze River IWM HU 45388

THE FAR EAST

ALTHOUGH THE DROPPING OF THE ATOMIC BOMBS on Hiroshima and Nagasaki in August 1945 hastened the surrender of Imperial Japan before HMS *Belfast*'s arrival in the Far East, she was still able to perform useful work in helping to evacuate the emaciated survivors of Japanese prisoner of war and civilian internment camps from Shanghai, China. These people – including entire families – had been made prisoners when the Japanese armed forces drove through the Far East in 1941.

In October 1945 the officers and men of HMS *Belfast* organised a party for the children in the camps. The ship's company set up swings and roundabouts, and the most popular item on the menu was chocolate, which some children had never seen or tasted. In short order, the crew searched their lockers and handed over as much chocolate as they could find.

HMS *Belfast* continued to perform peacekeeping duties in the region until the autumn of 1947, when she sailed back to Great Britain for a refit. Following the refit, she returned to the Far East in December 1948 as flagship of the Fifth Cruiser Squadron. By this time, China was in turmoil as the struggle between the Nationalist government and the Chinese Communist Party, led by <u>Mao Zedong</u>, moved towards its conclusion. In April 1949 the British <u>sloop</u> HMS *Amethyst* was disabled and blockaded in the Yangtze River by Communist shore batteries. Attempts to rescue the stricken vessel by HMS *London*, *Consort* and *Black Swan* failed with heavy loss of life, and the *Amethyst* was trapped in the Yangtze for six weeks until she managed to escape on the night of 30 July.

Although HMS *Belfast* was not actively involved in the crisis, she was the flagship of Commander-in-Chief, Far Eastern Station Admiral Sir Patrick Brind in Hong Kong, and all orders given to *Amethyst*'s temporary commander, Lieutenant-Commander J S Kerans, emanated from *Belfast*.

OPPOSITE PAGE: LEFT Ratings celebrating Christmas in Number 20 Mess on board *Belfast* in 1951. Throughout the Korean War, a significant proportion of the ship's company were National Servicemen. IWM HU 36593 RIGHT HMS *Belfast* firing a salvo from her 6-inch guns against enemy troop concentrations on the west coast of Korea IWM A 31890

THE KOREAN WAR

AT THE END OF THE SECOND WORLD WAR, the ancient kingdom of Korea was split between a hard-line Communist regime in the north and a more moderate government, supported by the United States, in the south. On 25 June 1950, the North Korean People's Army invaded South Korea. The United Nations Security Council voted to give aid to the south and, after halting the North Koreans around the port of Pusan, UN forces landed behind enemy lines at Inchon and quickly overran most of the country. In October 1950, however, Communist China entered the war and thousands of 'People's Volunteers' – six full armies – crossed into North Korea. UN troops were forced to retreat, and by the summer of 1951 both sides had settled down to a lengthy war of attrition along the line of the 38th Parallel. After two years of negotiations, a ceasefire brought the fighting to an end on 22 July 1953. No formal peace treaty has ever been signed.

HMS *Belfast* was amongst the very first British ships to go into action off Korea, bombarding in support of retreating South Korean and American troops only 11 days after the North Korean invasion. Working closely with Allied forces both naval and ashore, patrolling and shore bombardments were her main duties. She was well respected for the accuracy of her gunnery and became known to the Americans as 'that straight-shooting ship'. While serving in Korea, *Belfast* took part in an action that her crew later referred to as the Battle of Changni-Do. Captured on the night of 15 July 1952, Changni-Do was a strategically important island off the Korean coast.

Belfast was in company of HMS *Amethyst* and, using *Amethyst*'s boats, the island was reconnoitred and a bombardment set up. As evening came, both ships were taking fire from batteries on the mainland, but *Belfast*'s 6-inch guns soon silenced them. The following morning Allied troops landed, and, with the support of accurate fire from both ships and co-ordinated air strikes, the island was retaken that day.

On 27 September 1952, HMS *Belfast* sailed for home. *Belfast* spent no less than 404 days on active patrol during the Korean War. Her service was as long and arduous as that with the Home Fleet during the Second World War, as the icy weather conditions were often similar to those in the Arctic.

DURING THE CONFLICT, HMS BELFAST TRAVELLED 97,035 MILES, USED 60,000 TONS OF FUEL AND FIRED 7,816 ROUNDS OF 6-INCH AMMUNITION. HER CREW ATE 625 TONS OF POTATOES AND DRANK 10½ TONS OF TEA – AS WELL AS 56,000 PINTS OF RUM.

THE LAST YEARS AT SEA

BY THE TIME HMS BELFAST RETURNED FROM KOREA, the days of the big gun armoured warship were drawing to a close. However, the Royal Navy still needed a small number of cruisers to support its aircraft carriers and to serve as flagships on Foreign Stations. In 1956 HMS *Belfast* was taken in hand at Devonport Dockyard for extended refit and modernisation to prepare her for operations in the atomic age. A remodelled enclosed **Bridge**, extensive air conditioning, modern gunnery control systems and new lattice masts gave her the look visitors see today. In August 1959 she set sail once more for the Far East. Almost three years were to elapse before she returned to home waters.

Belfast's last years at sea were perhaps the happiest in her long and eventful life. For the ship's company, there was ample opportunity for relaxation in between peacetime exercises as well as a round of official visits to some of the world's most exotic ports. The winds of change had blown in, and over a handful of years the old British Empire was transformed into a Commonwealth of independent nation states.

As Britain said goodbye to its empire, the need for a large peacetime navy dwindled; it was clear that HMS *Belfast*'s sea-going days were numbered. In August 1963, following a final exercise in the Mediterranean, she was paid off into reserve for the last time before being reclassified as a harbour accommodation ship.

IN TRUST FOR THE NATION: THE SHIP AS A MUSEUM

IN MAY 1971, after 32 years of service during which she had steamed nearly half a million miles, the last of the Royal Navy's wartime cruisers was 'reduced to disposal' in preparation for sale and destruction by the ship-breakers.

Fortunately, help was at hand. As early as 1967, the Imperial War Museum had investigated the possibility of preserving a Second World War cruiser, but the government of the day had been reluctant to provide the necessary funding. Undeterred, the museum encouraged the formation of an independent trust led by one of HMS *Belfast*'s former captains, Rear-Admiral Sir Morgan Morgan-Giles. Eventually, this devoted band of enthusiasts succeeded in bringing her to London, where she opened to visitors on **Trafalgar Day**, 21 October 1971.

As of 2010, nearly 7 million people have visited the ship and have had a glimpse of what life was like in the Royal Navy during one of the most dramatic periods of British history. But, long after leaving naval service, the life of the ship continues.

IWM continues to preserve and present the ship through its dedicated team of staff and volunteers – many of them veteran crew – who make sure that HMS *Belfast* still has a role to play in reminding visitors of her own unique place in Britain's maritime heritage.

OPPOSITE PAGE: LEFT HMS *Belfast* anchored off Plymouth Devonport in July 1959 after her extended refit and modernisation. Her bridge superstructure was enlarged, modern radar and fire control systems fitted, and her anti-aircraft armament brought up to date. In addition, the accommodation for the ship's company was greatly improved. IWM A 34201 **RIGHT** Leaving Singapore in April 1962 at the end of her last Far Eastern service comission IWM HU 4646 **ABOVE** Alone and forlorn, the old cruiser lies in Fareham Creek, near Portsmouth, awaiting her final journey to the ship-breakers IWM MH 13768 **OVERLEAF** Nearly home. With her topmast just clearing the upper-works of Tower Bridge, HMS *Belfast* arrives in the Pool of London on 15 October 1971. IWM MH 15061

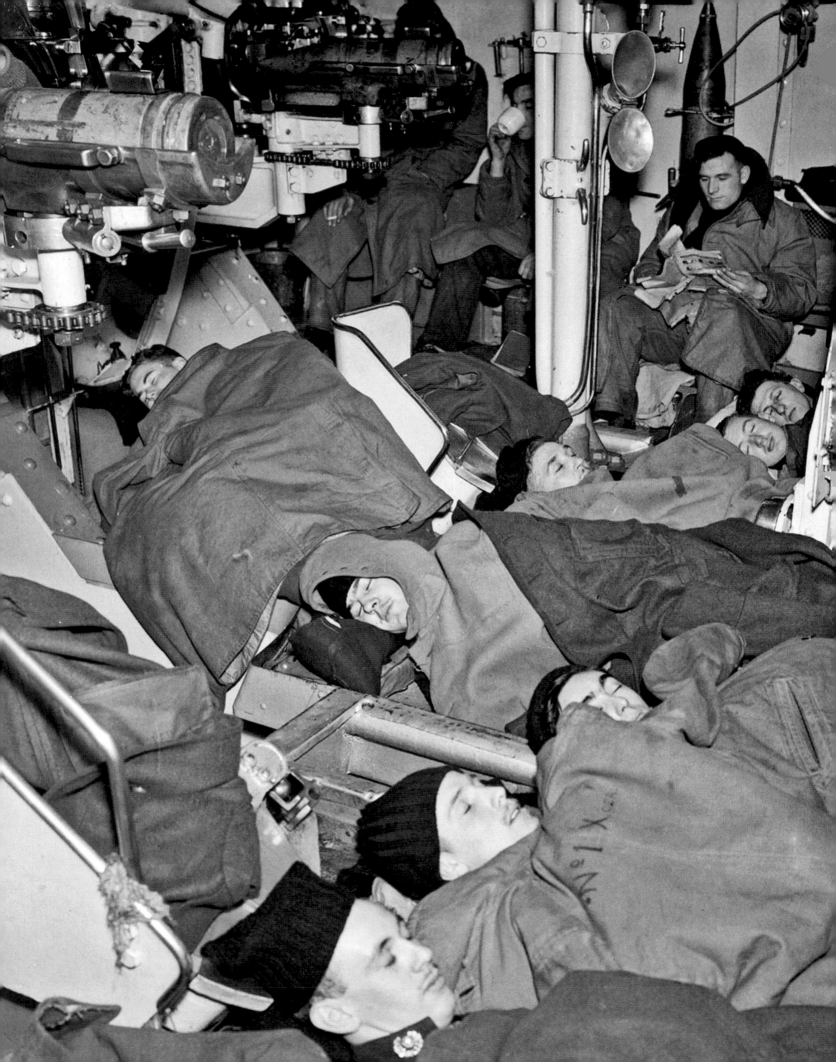

LIFE ON BOARD THE SHIP

**'THE BEST NIGHT'S SLEEP YOU'LL EVER HAVE!
IT'S A LOVELY SLEEP – YOU'RE ENCLOSED, YOU'RE COMFORTABLE –
ESPECIALLY WITH THE MOTION OF THE SHIP.'**

George Moody, Seaman during the Korean War

THE QUARTERDECK

TODAY THE <u>QUARTERDECK</u> IS THE MAIN ENTRANCE TO THE SHIP.
Officers and <u>ratings</u> always salute when stepping onto the
Quarterdeck of a Royal Naval vessel. It was here that flag
officers, captains of ships and others who were entitled
to the honour were 'piped' on board and where guards
and bands were paraded. The Quarterdeck was 'Officer
Country', and ratings were not normally permitted to set
foot on it except when on duty, for PT classes or to attend
the regular Sunday church services presided over by the
captain of the ship. This tradition of worship is maintained
each November when the Quarterdeck is the setting for
HMS *Belfast*'s annual Remembrance Day service.

PREVIOUS PAGES A Royal Marine gun crew sleeping in one of HMS *Sheffield*'s
6-inch gun turrets while on patrol in 1941, in order to be ready for
immediate action. *Sheffield* was a half-sister to HMS *Belfast* and the two
cruisers fought alongside eachother at the Battle of North Cape. IWM A
6879; Even the ship's cats had a hammock IWM SITE BELF 429 LEFT During
a visit to ships of the Home Fleet, the King (far right) shakes hands with
Captain Frederick Parham, commanding officer of HMS *Belfast*, as he
leaves the ship. *Belfast*'s company are present. In the foreground, the ships'
detachment of Royal Marines are gathered on the Quarterdeck. IWM A
18665 BELOW LEFT The silver bell on the Quarterdeck IWM SITE BELF 284
BELOW RIGHT Inside 'Y' Turret. Twenty-seven men worked in this cramped
space, each with his own job. IWM SITE BELF 376

THE SILVER BELL

HMS BELFAST'S SILVER BELL was presented by the people
of Belfast in October 1948. On the inner rim of the
bell are the names of the children born to serving
officers and sailors who were christened on board.
Traditionally, the upturned bell was used as a font. When
HMS *Belfast* was in service, the original ship's bell – which
is now in Northern Ireland – was sounded every half-hour
to mark the passing of each watch.

'Y' 6-INCH TURRET

OVERLOOKING THE QUARTERDECK ARE 'X' AND 'Y' TURRETS, the
<u>after</u> pair of HMS *Belfast*'s four 6-inch Mark XXIII Triple Gun
Turrets.

'Y' Turret is now the immersive *Gun Turret Experience*, which
recreates the atmosphere in the turret during the Battle of
North Cape (see page 16). It features a voice-over based on
recorded memories from the IWM oral history collection,
and special effects, including a moving floor.

Further information about the operation of the ship's 6-inch
guns can be found in the section of this guide relating to 'A'
Turret on page 52.

THE <u>WHITE ENSIGN</u> IS FLOWN DAY AND NIGHT BY ALL ROYAL NAVAL VESSELS AT SEA, AND FROM
'COLOURS' (8.00AM IN SUMMER, 9.00AM IN WINTER) TO SUNSET WHEN IN HARBOUR

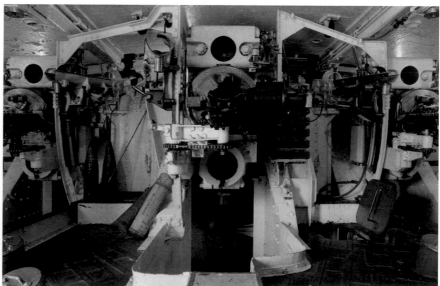

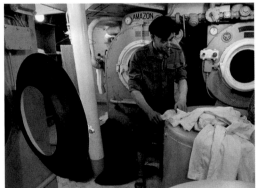

SHIP'S LAUNDRY AND 21-INCH TORPEDO

THROUGHOUT MOST OF HER ACTIVE LIFE, HMS *Belfast*'s crew were expected to wash (or '<u>dhobi</u>' in naval slang) their own clothes in buckets and basins. It was not until her extended refit and modernisation in the late 1950s that a well-equipped laundry was finally installed. When the ship was in the Far East, locally recruited Chinese workers were often employed as laundrymen and in other roles. Sadly, one of these workers, Leading <u>Steward</u> Lau So, was killed and four others were wounded when *Belfast* was struck by a Communist shore battery during the Korean War.

On the starboard side of the ship, next to the Laundry, is an example of a 21-inch Mark IX torpedo. HMS *Belfast* originally carried six of these weapons in two triple revolving mounts. The torpedo mountings were removed and their firing ports plated over during her refit in the 1950s.

SOUND REPRODUCTION EQUIPMENT ROOM AND CHAPEL

HMS BELFAST'S Sound Reproduction Equipment Room was used at the end of her active life to entertain the crew with popular music and radio programmes.

By tradition, all large Royal Navy warships have an area set aside as a chapel. The ship's chaplain was an important member of the crew, acting as a friend and adviser to sailors of all religious denominations. HMS *Belfast*'s Chapel is still occasionally used for christenings and for private worship.

THE SHIP'S COMPANY GALLEY AND CHIEF PETTY OFFICERS' MESSDECK

THE SHIP'S COMPANY <u>GALLEY</u> dates from the period after HMS *Belfast*'s modernisation, when meals for the crew were prepared by trained and qualified staff and served from the counter – a practice known as General or Cafeteria Messing. This system brought about a great improvement in the quality and variety of meals served in HM warships and reflected the improved living conditions expected by sailors in the post-war Navy.

Instead of taking meals in their individual messes, the crew now ate in a common canteen – the Ship's Company Dining Hall. The Galley staffs were supplemented by ratings from each department of the ship who were detailed to work in the Vegetable Preparation Room. Additional galleys serving the officers in the <u>Wardroom</u> and the Admiral's Dining Room were located further aft.

The Chief Petty Officers' <u>Mess</u>, located on the starboard side of the ship immediately opposite the Ship's Company Galley, is a typical example of the accommodation provided for HMS *Belfast*'s crew after her modernisation. The new facilities included bunks and lockers.

OPPOSITE: CLOCKWISE FROM TOP A 21-inch Mark IX torpedo being fired from one of the ship's triple torpedo mountings during sea trials in 1939 IWM HU 16022; General messing IWM A 19771; Sound Reproduction Equipment Room IWM SITE BELF 185; The ship's Laundry IWM SITE BELF 352 BELOW LEFT Board showing a typical menu from the 1960s IWM SITE BELF 430 BELOW RIGHT The Galley today IWM SITE BELF 195

MENU

MACARONI CHEESE

OR

FISH & CHIPS

WITH

PEAS & CARROTS

JAM ROLY POLY

OR

APPLE PIE

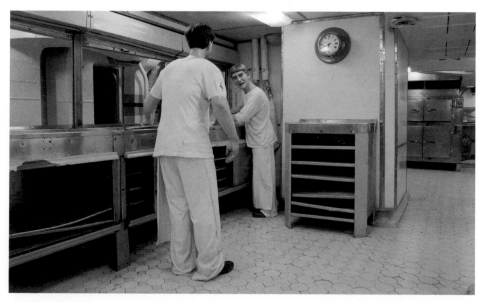

BAKERY AND BEEF SCREEN

JUST AFT OF THE CHIEF PETTY OFFICERS' MESSDECK are a number of compartments devoted to the provisioning of the ship in her last years of active service.

Stowage space in many of the ships which sailed in company with HMS *Belfast* during her service as flagship in the Far East was extremely limited, and she was constantly expected to act as 'mother' to her smaller charges, providing them with essential foodstuffs from her capacious stores. Each day a staff of six bakers had the mammoth task of producing sufficient bread not only for HMS *Belfast*'s crew, but also for the crews of smaller vessels which had no means of baking bread.

The Beef Screen served as the ship's butcher's shop. HMS *Belfast* was authorised to carry two trained Royal Marine butchers, who also kept an eye on the refrigerated Galley Ready Use Store.

SICKBAY AND DENTAL SURGERY

AS A CRUISER, HMS BELFAST WAS SPECIFICALLY DESIGNED TO SPEND LENGTHY PERIODS AT SEA, and it was essential that she should be adequately equipped to look after the health of her crew. In addition, she was expected to provide emergency services for smaller vessels, such as frigates and destroyers, which lacked all but the most rudimentary medical facilities.

Following modernisation, HMS *Belfast* was authorised to carry a medical complement of two officers and up to five sick-berth attendants, including a radiographer and physiotherapist. The operating theatre was sufficiently well equipped, complete with its own small X-ray machine, for the surgeon-commander to perform most routine operations, but it was normally only used in emergencies because of the movement and vibration of the ship. No such inhibitions seem to have affected the work of his deputy, the dental officer.

BETWEEN MAY 1959 AND OCTOBER 1960, 52 FOUR-POUND (1.8 KG) LOAVES AND 1,440 ROLLS WERE PRODUCED EVERY DAY. DURING THIS PERIOD THEY ALSO MADE A TOTAL OF 10 MILES OF SAUSAGES.

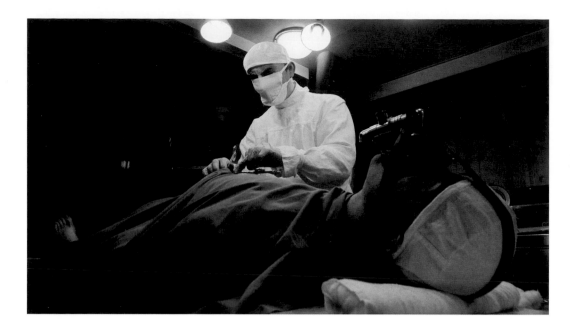

OPPOSITE PAGE: LEFT Kneading machine in the Bakery IWM SITE BELF 418 **RIGHT** One of HMS *Belfast's* Royal Marine butchers at work in the Beef Screen IWM SITE BELF 194
LEFT The surgeon-commander carries out an emergency operation in the ship's operating theatre IWM SITE BELF 206
BELOW The dental officer was usually a surgeon lieutenant-commander and was an important member of the ship's general medical team, but his main task was to look after the dental health of the ship's company IWM SITE BELF 200

'DURING THIS EXERCISE, OUR CHINESE BARBER, LAI SUM, WAS SUDDENLY TAKEN ILL WITH AN INTERNAL HAEMORRHAGE. HE WAS GIVEN A TRANSFUSION IN THE SICK BAY, WHILE WE DASHED OFF TOWARDS OKINAWA AND A US NAVY HELICOPTER DASHED OUT FROM OKINAWA TO MEET US.'

HMS *Belfast* 1959–1961 Commission Book

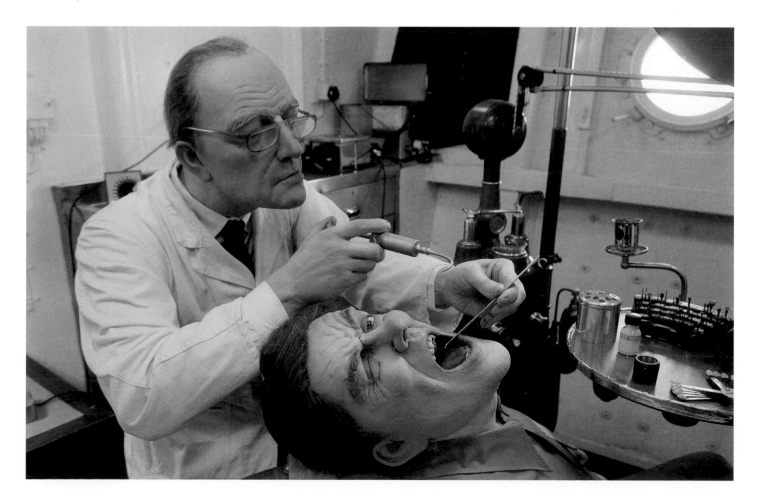

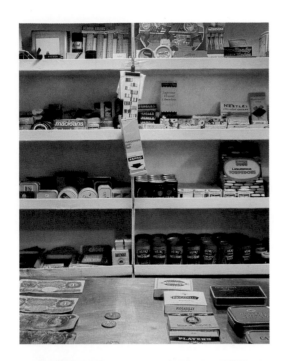

PROVISION ISSUE ROOM

FOR MANY OF HMS BELFAST'S CREW, the Provision Issue Room was the most important compartment in the entire ship, for it was here that the daily rum ration was measured and prepared for issue in a ritual dating back to the middle of the eighteenth century.

RUM HAD BEEN A REGULAR PART OF THE ROYAL NAVY'S DIET SINCE THE CAPTURE OF JAMAICA IN 1655. ORIGINALLY, SAILORS RECEIVED NO LESS THAN HALF A PINT A DAY OF NEAT SPIRIT, BUT IN 1740 ADMIRAL EDWARD VERNON INTRODUCED THE ISSUE OF GROG (TWO PARTS WATER TO ONE PART RUM), WHICH REMAINED ONE OF THE GREAT TRADITIONS OF NAVAL LIFE UNTIL AS LATE AS 1970.

NAAFI CANTEEN

SINCE 1921, the Navy Army and Air Force Institute's (NAAFI) Naval Canteen Service has served the Royal Navy both ashore and afloat. Large warships such as HMS *Belfast* were equipped with well-stocked canteens selling a wide variety of goods, including duty-free tobacco, confectionery and small luxury items, as well as essentials such as toothpaste and shoe polish. Wine and spirits were not permitted, but, from 1960 onwards, each member of the crew could purchase up to two cans of beer a day, provided the cans were opened immediately to prevent hoarding. A percentage of the profits generated from this enterprise went towards a general ship's social fund, known as the Canteen Fund, administered by a committee for the benefit of the whole crew.

ARCTIC MESSDECKS

WHEN HMS BELFAST WAS FIRST COMMISSIONED, a sailor's life was in many respects little changed from the days of Nelson. Sailors joined the Navy at 16 and signed initially for a 12-year engagement, starting from the age of 18. Pay for an <u>able seaman</u> was just 21 shillings (£28.55 today) per week, out of which married men were required to make an allowance of 3 shillings and sixpence (£4.54) to their wives. A sailor received an additional 12 shillings and sixpence (£14.92) for each child, and a marriage allowance of 18 shillings (£23.36) per week was paid directly to his wife while he was at sea. Even allowing for the lower cost of living, the wages of an able seaman were barely sufficient to keep his family above the poverty line.

Like their predecessors in Nelson's time, HMS *Belfast*'s ratings lived, slept and ate in communal areas known as messes, which were crammed into every available space. While officers were allocated cabins, the ratings slung their hammocks in their mess or slept where they could around the ship. Despite the fact that hammocks were slung only 21 inches (52 cm) apart, the hugely enlarged crews required in wartime (HMS *Belfast*'s authorised peacetime complement of 761 had increased to over 950 by the end of the Second World War) meant that it was not at all unusual for men on different watches to share the use of a hammock or to sleep on the deck beneath one of the mess tables.

Until the 1950s, large warships such as HMS *Belfast* operated a catering system known as Broadside Messing. Each mess would appoint a duty cook to help prepare the basic meal for his messmates in the Galley, take it to his mess, serve it and wash up before returning the empty containers to the galley. Each mess had an allowance to purchase additional or 'luxury' items of food, and the ship's supply officer – the '<u>Pusser</u>' – would present an account for payment at the end of each month. Naval food was stodgy and unimaginative, but there was generally plenty of it, and many messes preferred to save up their allowance for a first-class binge when they had the opportunity to go ashore.

OPPOSITE: CLOCKWISE FROM TOP LEFT NAAFI Canteen IWM SITE BELF 433; 'Up Spirits!' The rum ration is issued to each mess. IWM A 1777; Hammocks in the Arctic Messdeck. The red lighting – 'darken ship routine' – is intended to preserve the crew's night vision when in action and to ensure HMS *Belfast* showed no bright lights which might betray her position to the enemy. IWM SITE BELF 435 LEFT Broadside Messing. After collecting the dinner for his mess from the Galley, a Royal Marine duty mess cook ladles out his mates' portions at the communal table. IWM A 16299

CAPSTAN MACHINERY SPACE AND PUNISHMENT CELL

THE CAPSTAN MACHINERY SPACE is situated almost in the **bow** of the ship and contains the electric motors, gears and vertical shafts which drove the capstans on the **Fo'c'sle** above. Wooden capstan bars, stowed overhead, were used to turn the capstans by hand in the event of a mechanical breakdown. Despite this mass of machinery, the compartment was home to 33 sailors, a clear indication of the lack of suitable living space for *Belfast's* crew at the height of her operational service.

AT THE FORWARD END of this compartment are the ship's punishment cells. The captain had the power to sentence offenders to periods of up to 14 days' imprisonment for offences such as sleeping on watch, drunkenness or leave-breaking.

While serving in the North Atlantic during the Second World War, it was not unusual for HMS *Belfast* to encounter hurricane conditions with waves up to 50 feet high. Standing in the Capstan Machinery Space, one can imagine what it must have been like to live in this compartment as the ship struggled to lift her bow from beneath the great masses of water foaming over her Fo'c'sle before plunging down to meet the shock of yet another mountainous wave.

BELOW Slung hammocks in the Capstan Machinery Space IWM SITE BELF 440
RIGHT Arctic gale, 1943. It was not uncommon for waves to reach above the height of the ship's bridge. IWM HU 9144

THE INNER WORKINGS

'FUELLING HAD ITS LIGHTER MOMENTS, SUCH AS THE DAY P.O.M. (E) DALE, COVERED WITH FUEL, LOOKED INTO HQ2 AND REPORTED "A1 TANK 101% FULL, SIR!" ALSO THE OCCASION WHEN THE FUEL HOSE SOMEHOW ENTERED THE SCUTTLE OF THE CAPTAIN'S SECRETARY'S OFFICE!'

HMS *Belfast* 1961–1962 Commission Book

SHELL ROOMS AND MAGAZINES

THE SHELL ROOMS AND <u>MAGAZINES</u> ARE LOCATED WELL BELOW THE SHIP'S WATERLINE and are the most heavily protected of all the ship's compartments. Apart from the vertical protection against shell-fire provided by the main armour belt, 4.5 inches (114 mm) thick, the deck immediately above the Shell Rooms is also armoured to a thickness of 3 inches (76 mm) to provide protection against aerial bombs.

Each of the 6-inch Gun Turrets is served by its own Shell Room and Magazine, with the Magazines and their vulnerable cordite charges sited below the Shell Rooms on the Hold Deck, the lowest of all HMS *Belfast*'s seven habitable decks. The shells and cordite charges were sent up to the turrets above by mechanical hoists.

In the event of HMS *Belfast* receiving a hit which threatened an explosion in the Magazines, the compartments could be rapidly flooded to prevent the loss of the ship. In such circumstances, the men working in the Handling Rooms would have had little chance of escape.

SIX-INCH TRANSMITTING STATION

THE TRANSMITTING STATION WAS A VITAL COMPONENT in the complex system which controlled the operation of HMS *Belfast*'s main armament. The Transmitting Station housed the Admiralty Fire Control Table (AFCT), a mechanical computer designed in the 1930s. Information provided by the Forward Director Control Tower on the Bridge about the range and <u>bearing</u> of an enemy ship was fed into the AFCT, which then calculated the correct angles of train and elevation required for the guns in all four turrets to hit their target.

A smaller version of the AFCT, known as the Admiralty Fire Control Clock, provided similar data for the after turrets only.

PREVIOUS PAGE Replica 6-inch shells IWM SITE BELF 242; Engine Room Telegraph IWM SITE BELF 347 **BELOW** This very rare photograph of Royal Marines manning a transmitting station in action was taken on board the aircraft carrier HMS *Victorious* during the Second World War IWM A 7640 **RIGHT** The Admiralty Fire Control Table IWM SITE BELF 423

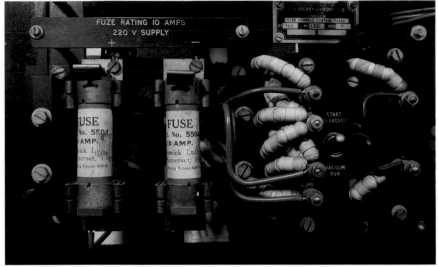

IWM SITE BELF 267

IWM SITE BELF 256

IWM SITE BELF 422

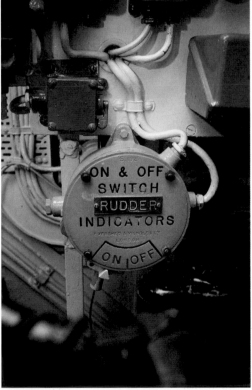

IWM SITE BELF 264

IWM SITE BELF 266

IWM SITE BELF 255

IWM SITE BELF 260

IWM SITE BELF 263

IWM SITE BELF 218

IWM SITE BELF 220

FORWARD CONVERSION MACHINERY ROOM

HMS BELFAST USED BOTH DIRECT (DC) AND ALTERNATING (AC) ELECTRIC CURRENT to power her equipment. The AC current, which supplied her gyro compass, gunnery control systems, radar and wireless equipment, was converted in this compartment and distributed from the switchboard on the other side of the 6-inch Transmitting Station.

FORWARD GYRO COMPASS ROOM

THE NAVIGATION COMPASS in this compartment worked on gyroscopic principles which ensured that whichever way the ship turned the compass always pointed true north. This allowed the ship to be steered accurately and also provided the directional basis for aligning the radars and the gunnery control systems.

FORWARD STEERING POSITION

HMS BELFAST WAS STEERED from this heavily protected compartment by the ship's helmsman, who received his instructions from the officer of the watch on the Compass Platform. The steering motors and the massive hydraulic rams which operated the ship's rudder are located beneath the Quarterdeck in the Tiller Flat, where the emergency backup steering position is also located.

The ship's telephone exchange is housed at the back of the compartment.

LEFT Details of machinery from around the ship BELOW HMS *Belfast*'s Forward Steering Position. A secondary emergency steering position is located near the Tiller Flat at the stern of the ship. IWM SITE BELF 431

BOILER ROOMS

HMS BELFAST'S MAIN PROPULSIVE MACHINERY is laid out according to a system first introduced by the United States Navy known as <u>unit propulsion</u>. This system is based upon the grouping together of the boilers and engines into self-contained units – in HMS *Belfast*'s case, four boilers and four engines arranged in pairs (Boiler Room/Engine Room, Boiler Room/Engine Room) in four separate but cross-connected watertight compartments – so that a single hit from an enemy shell or torpedo could never disable more than 50 per cent of the ship's power plant.

FORWARD BOILER ROOM

THE ENTRANCE TO THE FORWARD BOILER ROOM is guarded by a double set of doors that form an airlock to the huge compartment beyond. This was essential as any sudden change in air pressure could result in the boilers '<u>flashing back</u>' and incinerating anything, or anyone, immediately outside them. Once through these doors, crew members descended through a maze of pipework and trunking to the floor of the Boiler Room, three decks below.

HMS *Belfast*'s boilers burned a heavy oil mixture, known as furnace fuel oil, to produce super-heated steam at a pressure of 350 pounds per square inch. The steam was then piped through to the turbine engines, which in turn drove the propeller shafts.

Each boiler consisted of three drums; the two lower drums contained water, which was passed through the furnace in steel tubes. The steam generated was collected in the third drum on the top of the boiler. Steam was also used to drive the ship's turbo-generators, providing *Belfast* with electric power while at sea.

Other auxiliary machinery in this compartment includes the fire and <u>bilge</u> pump, which drew sea water into the ship's fire mains and pumped out the bilge beneath the machinery.

HMS BELFAST CARRIED 2,256 TONS OF FUEL OIL AND HER MAXIMUM SPEED WAS 32 KNOTS (59 KM/H) ON FULL POWER

LEFT AND BELOW Quiet today, the ship's boiler rooms were hot, deafening places producing enough power for a small town
IWM SITE BELF 249; IWM SITE BELF 336; IWM SITE BELF 248

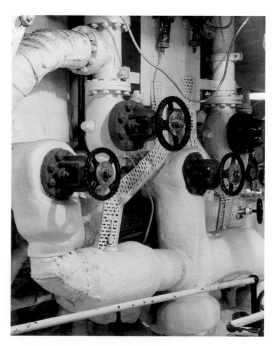

SHIP'S COMPANY WASHROOMS

BETWEEN THE FORWARD BOILER ROOM AND FORWARD ENGINE ROOM are the crew's washrooms and showers. These facilities were added after the refit in the 1950s. There is also an emergency exit leading back up to the Upper Deck.

FORWARD ENGINE ROOM

HMS BELFAST HAS FOUR PROPELLER SHAFTS, the two outer ones driven by the engines in the Forward Engine Room and the inner ones driven by the engines in the After Engine Room. Each of the four turbine engines is capable of generating 20,000 shaft horsepower, making a total of 80,000 shp (an average family car develops 100 hp) – enough to drive HMS *Belfast* through the water at 32 <u>knots</u> (59 km/h).

Each engine has four distinct turbine rotors: the two large high and low pressure turbines, which worked in series to develop full power ahead; a small cruising turbine for more economical speeds; and an <u>astern</u> reverse turbine. The super-heated steam from the boilers could be directed to the desired combination of rotors by means of control throttles, driving the turbines, which in turn drove the propeller shafts through the gearbox mechanism attached to each engine.

The auxiliary machinery in this compartment includes a steam-powered turbo-generator and a set of twin evaporators, which were used to distil sea water for the boilers and for domestic purposes.

BELOW LEFT Ship's Company Washrooms IWM SITE BELF 421 **BELOW RIGHT** Engine Room detail IWM SITE BELF 250 **RIGHT** The Forward Engine Room IWM SITE BELF 253

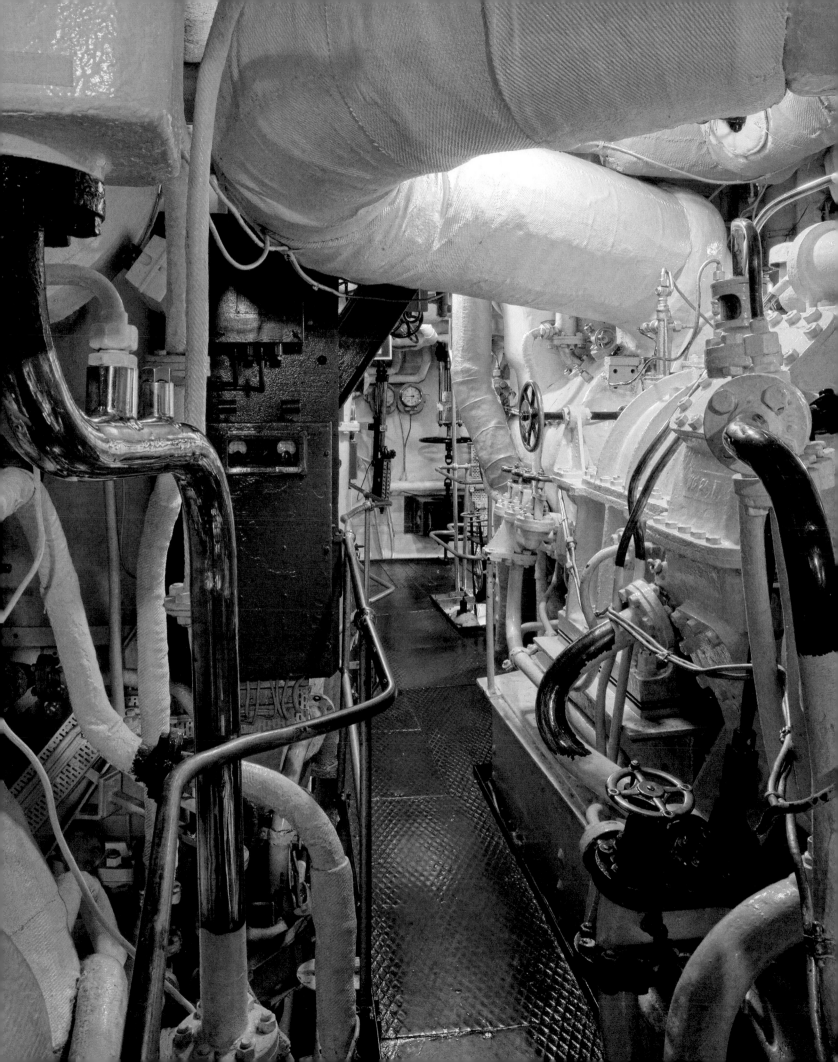

ACTION STATIONS!

'WE WENT DOWN ALL THESE FLIGHTS OF STEPS. I SAID, "WHERE ARE WE GOING?"
HE SAID, "WE'RE GOING TO YOUR ACTION STATION." "WHAT, DOWN HERE?" HE SAID,
"YEP, THE ASDIC CABINET IS DOWN ON THE BILGE PLATES." AND I THOUGHT, "CRIKEY!"
AND I TRIED TO COUNT THE NUMBER OF LADDERS AND THE NUMBER OF STEPS I
WENT DOWN, AND I THOUGHT, "I'LL HAVE TO GET TREMENDOUSLY FIT TO GET DOWN
ALL THESE THINGS, BUT AT LEAST I WON'T NEED A DUFFLE COAT DOWN HERE!"'

Bob Shrimpton on being shown to his action station
on the ASDIC (submarine detection equipment)
on his first day on board

FO'C'SLE AND ANCHORS

THE FORECASTLE, OR FO'C'SLE, was originally a raised platform on wooden warships where fighting men would gather to rain down fire upon the decks of enemy ships below. In more recent times the Fo'c'sle has been used primarily for the operation of ship's anchors. HMS *Belfast* originally carried three anchors, two on the starboard bow and one on the port. One of the starboard anchors (the sheet anchor) was removed in 1940, and now only the port anchor (weighing 5.5 tons) is stowed on the deck. The anchor cables pass around the cable-holders before disappearing into the Cable Locker below.

HMS *Belfast*'s anchors were usually raised and lowered by electric power, but in an emergency large wooden bars could be inserted into the capstan to operate the machinery manually. It took the combined efforts of 144 men to raise the ship's anchors by this method. Today, HMS *Belfast* is permanently moored to the river bed, but she still rises and falls about 20 feet (6–7 m) every day as the tides ebb and flood.

In common with all Royal Naval vessels in harbour, HMS *Belfast* flies the Union Jack daily between 'Colours' and sunset from the jack-staff at her bow.

'A' TURRET

THE FURTHEST FORWARD of HMS *Belfast*'s four 6-inch Mark XXIII Triple Gun Turrets, 'A' and 'B', dominate the Fo'c'sle. Each of HMS *Belfast*'s heavily armoured turrets weighs 175 tons and had a crew of 27 working in the turret gun house. A further 22 men worked in the Shell Rooms and Magazines located beneath each turret. The shells and the cordite charges which propelled them were sent up to the gun house by mechanical hoists, where they were rammed into the gun breeches by hand. The guns could be used against enemy targets at sea or on land and had a maximum range of approximately 14 miles (22 km).

The guns in both forward turrets are trained and elevated onto a target some 12.5 miles (20 km) away in north-west London, the London Gateway Services on the M1 – a reminder of the awesome power of naval gunnery in the Second World War.

ADMIRAL'S BRIDGE

HMS BELFAST WAS BUILT AS A FLAGSHIP and carried an admiral for most of her operational life. This additional bridge was provided so that the admiral and his staff could exercise control over the fleet or squadron of vessels under his command without overcrowding the Compass Platform and interfering with the operation of the ship.

BRIDGE WIRELESS OFFICE

ON THE SAME LEVEL AS THE BRIDGE WINGS is the Bridge Wireless Office (BWO), where all incoming radio messages were received and outgoing messages transmitted. The BWO is still used today by the Royal Naval Amateur Radio Society, and enthusiasts can contact them on HMS *Belfast* by using the ship's international call sign, GB2RN. The Electronic Warfare Office, which housed equipment designed to confuse enemy radar and radio signals, is located next to the BWO.

On the deck above are the Flag Deck, Gunnery Direction Platform and, overlooking them, the Foremast and Forward Director Control Tower.

The entire forward superstructure was extensively rebuilt in the 1950s refit, and all the visible equipment dates from this period.

FLAG DECK AND FOREMAST

THE FLAG DECK WAS USED to send visual signals to nearby vessels. The 10-inch and 20-inch signalling projectors on either side of the deck flashed messages in Morse code, and the Foremast was used to hoist flag signals. HMS *Belfast* was originally equipped with lightweight tripod masts, but these were replaced by much stronger lattice masts in order to support the weight of the radar systems fitted to the ship after modernisation.

FORWARD DIRECTOR CONTROL TOWER

THE FORWARD DIRECTOR CONTROL TOWER (DCT) controlled the operation of all four of HMS *Belfast*'s 6-inch gun turrets. Originally, the DCT was fitted with a large <u>optical range finder</u>, but from 1942 onwards targets were normally acquired and tracked by radar.

A second DCT, mounted on the after superstructure, was provided to control the independent operation of the two after turrets.

GUN DIRECTION PLATFORM

IN GOOD VISIBILITY, all of HMS *Belfast*'s guns could be controlled from the Gun Direction Platform (GDP) at the forward end of the upper bridge. The captain's sight on the centre platform was used to indicate targets to the Director Control Tower, and the GDP offered an unrivalled vantage point for lookouts manning the four circular sights to search the sea and sky with their binoculars.

OPERATIONS ROOM AND COMPASS PLATFORM

HMS BELFAST'S OPERATIONS ROOM and compass platform are the central nervous system of the entire ship. Both of these areas were refitted in the 1950s, and thus the layout and equipment differ from the ship's Second World War fittings. In the Operations Room, information derived from radar, <u>sonar</u> and intelligence reports on Allied and enemy surface, submarine and air forces was collated and displayed on plots and 'stateboards'. From this combined information, the captain was able to evaluate the tactical situation and respond accordingly. The room is reconstructed to show HMS *Belfast*'s role in large overseas live fire training exercises, such as Operation 'Pony Express', a multi-national exercise near Borneo, 1961.

It was from the Compass Platform that the captain or officer of the watch controlled the ship at sea, passing steering and engine orders to the helmsman at the wheel in the Forward Steering Position, located six decks below. The ship's course was plotted by the navigating officer and his assistants in the Charthouse at the back of the Compass Platform.

Recent renovations have brought this area to life, getting you closer to the equipment and even allowing you to plot your own operation to retrieve a downed helicopter at sea.

CLOCKWISE FROM TOP LEFT The Flag Deck was controlled by the yeoman of signals, who would pass messages to other vessels in sight using flags, semaphore or Morse code on a signal projector. In this picture taken on board HMS *Sheffield* in 1941, ice is forming on the projector, making the signalman's task extremely difficult. IWM IWM A 6872; **Detail of compass binnacle** IWM SITE BELF 225; The Operations Room on the aircraft carrier HMS *Victorious*, 1965 IWM GOV 13331; **LEFT** View of the refitted Compass Platform in 1959. Before the refit, HMS *Belfast* possessed an open bridge. IWM MH 28668

OFFICERS' SEA CABINS

ON THE DECK BELOW the Compass Platform are the sea cabins reserved for the admiral, his staff and the captain. These were provided in addition to their day cabins, located beneath the Quarterdeck, so that they could work and sleep in close proximity to the Admiral's Bridge and Compass Platform when the ship was in action or taking part in exercises. Additional sea cabins a further deck below were given to less senior officers.

FOUR-INCH GUNS

HMS BELFAST'S SECONDARY BATTERY of four twin 4-inch HA/LA Mark XIX mountings is located in pairs on either side of the ship between her funnels. During the Second World War, HMS *Belfast* carried six of these mountings, but the aftermost pair was removed at the end of the war to make way for additional deckhouses. Although they were primarily designed to protect the ship from attack by enemy aircraft, the guns could also be used against surface targets, hence the designation HA/LA – High Angle/Low Angle.

BOAT DECK AND MAIN MAST

DIRECTLY IN FRONT OF THE FORWARD PAIR of 4-inch mountings lies the great open expanse of HMS *Belfast's* Boat Deck. When in commission, *Belfast* carried a large number of ship's boats, which were hoisted in and out of the water by the 7-ton electric boat crane mounted just aft of the Bridge.

In the early stages of the Second World War, however, the Boat Deck was used as a platform for Supermarine Walrus reconnaissance seaplanes, which could be launched by catapult to search for vessels beyond the horizon. After completing a mission, the aircraft would land in the sea alongside the ship and be lifted back on board by crane. HMS *Belfast* normally carried two machines, each of which was provided with a weather-proof hangar in the wings of the Bridge. Once the ship had been fitted with long-range search radar there was no further need to carry aircraft on board, and in mid 1943 the seaplanes were removed.

BELOW LEFT The fixed ammunition shells for *Belfast's* 4-inch HA/LA mountings weighed 66 pounds (30 kg) and were loaded manually into the breeches of the guns. The shells had to be punched home with a clenched fist, as the breech blocks closed automatically and could easily crush the fingers of an open hand. A well-trained gun crew was expected to be able to maintain an average rate of fire of ten rounds per minute per gun. IWM A 16317
BELOW RIGHT HMS *Belfast's* Seaplane Flight, 700 Squadron Fleet Air Arm, pictured in front of one of the ship's Supermarine Walrus Mark I amphibians IWM HU 447700 **RIGHT** A typical officers' sea cabin IWM SITE BELF 357

CONSERVATION

TAKING INTO ACCOUNT the safety of visitors and staff, the availability of appropriate materials and their cost, conserving HMS *Belfast* in her present condition is a delicate balance. The aim of the various conservation projects is to present the ship as she would have appeared during the final part of her working life in the Royal Navy, following her 1959 modernisation refit. The ship has undergone many refits since her launch in March 1938, but some fixtures and fittings still date back to this time. Conservation work is carried out by the ship's technicians, who are supplemented by a team of volunteers.

Where possible traditional methods are used for all work, referring to period technical handbooks, drawings and photographs to ensure that the ship is presented in an historically accurate context.

Conservation and restoration projects are currently in hand to preserve the secondary and close range weapon systems and their respective directors. Longer term plans include the conservation of Upper Deck winches and the boat crane. These are particularly important since they are exposed to the elements, and as with any steel structure, the biggest threat is from corrosion.

In addition to large-scale restoration work, the ship's technical staff are also responsible for the daily upkeep of the ship, as well as operating and maintaining the live systems needed to run a successful museum. For instance, the ever-popular 'Kip in a Ship' messes were installed, and continue to be maintained by the team.

Conservation is an ongoing process; the hard work of staff and volunteers will mean that the ship remains a popular historic attraction for many years to come.

LEFT HMS *Belfast* in dry dock, 1982 IWM 1982 40 40
BELOW LEFT Technical Staff repairing corrosion damage to a Bridge Wing
BELOW RIGHT Warship Conservation Volunteers refitting a Fuse Unit during conservation of a four inch gun mount

GLOSSARY

Able Seaman A fully trained seaman with some experience, as opposed to an inexperienced Ordinary Seaman.

After Towards the rear part of a ship, as opposed to 'forward', which is towards the front (bow).

Astern Towards the back, or behind a ship altogether. Alternatively, to 'steam astern' is to steam in reverse.

Barracuda British naval torpedo and dive bomber. Entering service in 1943, it had a crew of three and a top speed of 385 kilometres per hour (240 mph).

Bearing Horizontal direction to a target, identified using a compass, eg. 'Bearing 045 degrees'.

Bilge The lowest compartment in a ship, where the two sides join above the keel. Often a receptacle for noxious water drained from other parts of the ship.

Bombing-Up Loading an aircraft with bombs.

Bow The pointed front end of a ship.

Bridge The area from which the captain commands a ship. Originates from the raised 'bridge' between the paddle wheels in early steam ships.

Broadside Firing all of a ship's main armament simultaneously. Originates from sailing warships, when ships' guns were mounted along the side and not in revolving turrets.

Capstan Revolving machinery used for raising and lowering anchors.

Compass Platform The magnetic compass originally had to be sited in the open to avoid interference caused by the surrounding steel. HMS *Belfast*'s Compass Platform is now enclosed, and the term is interchangeable with 'Bridge.'

Destroyers Small, fast warships armed with guns and torpedoes. The name evolved from the early twentieth-century term 'torpedo boat destroyer'.

Dhobi Slang term for laundry, from the Hindi word for 'washerman'.

Displacement A ship's bulk, expressed as the amount of water its hull pushes away, or displaces.

Flashing Back A sudden change in air pressure in the boiler room, resulting in the boiler doors being sucked open and a dangerous burst of flame.

Fo'c'sle The open deck at the bow of a ship and the seamen's living quarters below. Originates from early sailing warships, which had a raised platform for archers known as the 'forecastle'.

Frigates Originally lightly armed, fast sailing warships, frigates were small, simple anti-submarine ships during the Second World War. Today they are sophisticated multipurpose warships.

Galley A ship's kitchen.

Gyro Compass A compass that uses an electric, fast-spinning wheel (a gyroscope) to find true north, rather than magnetic north. Being less susceptible to magnetic fields caused by steel, they are particularly suitable for use in ships.

Gyroscopic Principles See above.

Helmsman Seaman responsible for steering a ship using the ship's wheel.

Hydraulic Ram A type of pump.

Knot A unit of speed equal to one nautical mile (1,852 m) per hour.

Magazines Secure, well-armoured space below the waterline for storing explosive charges used to fire shells from a ship's guns.

Mao Zedong Chinese Communist leader who took control of China in 1949 and ruled it until his death in 1976.

Mess Ratings lived, slept and ate together in groups known as 'messes'. The compartments in which these groups lived were known as 'messdecks', and the naval verb for both living and eating in them was 'messing'.

Officer of the Watch An officer on duty and responsible for the safe operation of an aspect of a ship's function, usually navigation.

Optical Range Finder Instrument used to measure distance.

Port and Starboard Early ships were steered by a 'steer-board' (large oar) sited over the right-hand side of the stern, which became known as the starboard side. This meant that in port the other side had to lie alongside the jetty, becoming known as the 'port' side.

Propulsive Having the power to propel.

Pusser Corruption of 'Purser', the officer in charge of supply. Consequently, anything issued by the Navy became known as 'Pusser's'. For example, 'Pusser's Kye' was slang for naval hot chocolate.

Quarterdeck The aftermost part of the Upper Deck, usually reserved for officers.

Radar Acronym for 'Radio Direction and Ranging'. Radio waves are bounced off objects back to a detecting source, providing the target's range, direction and height.

Range Distance to a target.

Rating An enlisted man in the Royal Navy, whatever his branch.

Rudder A vertically hinged metal plate below the stern of a ship used for steering.

Salvo Simultaneous discharge of a number of guns.

Sloop Originally a small sailing ship. During the Second World War the term was revived to describe small, simple anti-submarine vessels, but today it is no longer used for warships.

Sonar Acronym for 'Sound Navigation and Ranging'. Sound waves are bounced off submarines and echo with a characteristic 'ping'. The time between the transmission and the ping indicates the depth of the target. In the Royal Navy, sonar was originally known as ASDIC, an acronym for 'Anti-Submarine Detection Investigation Committee'.

Sortie A combat mission, usually by ships or aircraft.

Stern The blunt back end of a ship.

Steward Rating from the Supply and Secretariat Branch responsible for administering and distributing food, clothing, soap and tobacco. Other stewards serve in the officers' Wardroom.

Tiller Flat Any specific section of a ship containing several compartments is known as a 'flat'. The Tiller Flat is the location of the ship's wheel.

Trafalgar Day 21 October, the anniversary of the Battle of Trafalgar (1805), which was fought between a British fleet commanded by Vice-Admiral Horatio Lord Nelson, who was killed, and the combined fleets of France and Spain.

Trajectory The path of a shell fired from a gun.

Unit Propulsion Each propeller is driven by a self-contained unit of one turbine and one boiler, so that if one or more units are disabled a ship can still operate.

Walrus Single-engine amphibious biplane reconnaissance aircraft carried by British cruisers and battleships. Introduced in 1935, it had a crew of three and a top speed of 217 kilometres per hour (135 mph).

Wardroom The officers' mess in a naval ship or shore establishment.

White Ensign Flag flown by Royal Navy warships in commission, a red St George's Cross on a white field with a Union Flag in the upper canton. Originally Blue and Red Ensigns were also used, depending on the rank of the flag officer in command, but this practice ended in 1864.

LEARNING

DISCOVER A UNIQUE HISTORIC ENVIRONMENT. Film, photographs, objects and veteran testimonies tell the story of what life was like living and working on board HMS *Belfast* during her duties in the Second World War, the Cold War, Korea and beyond.

A visit to HMS *Belfast* can support the study of History, Literacy, Numeracy, Art, Science and Citizenship. Explore the ship on a self-directed visit, or for a charge add a learning session during term time.

A packed-lunch area capable of seating 30 children can be pre-booked, and there is additional space on the Upper Deck for picnics in fine weather.

Schools and youth groups can take part in *Belfast*'s Kip in a Ship programme and spend up to three nights on board the ship, sleeping in the restored 1950s messdecks and experiencing life below decks. Visit the website for more details.

Free drop-in family activities take place on most weekends and during school holidays. Full details are available on the website. For further information visit the learning pages at **iwm.org.uk/visits/hms-belfast/groups-schools**. If you would like to discuss your requirements please email **learningbookings@iwm.org.uk**.

SHOPPING

ENJOY BROWSING our large selection of gifts including books, models, posters and souvenirs for all ages. Our shop is situated on the Quayside at the entrance to the ship, so why not make a purchase during your visit. You can also shop online at **iwm.org.uk** and all your purchases support IWM.

CORPORATE AND PRIVATE HOSPITALITY AND EVENTS

HMS BELFAST IS AN IMPRESSIVE AND UNUSUAL corporate hospitality venue available for hire at competitive rates. Moored in a prime location between London Bridge and Tower Bridge, HMS *Belfast* contains nine decks of living history and offers delegates a completely unique experience.

There are several corporate spaces available for a variety of events, including boardroom meetings for 20 guests, conferences or banquets for 150, and spectacular parties for up to 450 guests during the summer on the outside decks.

Exclusive caterers Sodexo Prestige can provide tailor-made packages, including fresh modern classics, traditional naval food and beverages, 1940s-style actors and singers, and private tours by HMS *Belfast* staff or veterans.

With all this and more, it's almost easy to forget the stunning views from the ship's function rooms, where portholes look out onto the River Thames. Into the evening, as the lights of London flicker to life, there's no better place to view the city than from the deck of HMS *Belfast*.

Choosing HMS *Belfast* not only guarantees a truly one-of-a-kind venue for conferences, meetings, dinners or parties, but also excellent service and professional event management. No matter what event you are looking to hold, if it is important to you, it is important to HMS *Belfast*.

To book, simply call **020 3116 4457** or email **hms.belfast@sodexo.com**.

REFRESHMENTS

OUR NEW CAFÉ BAR is situated at the entrance to the ship. Open daily for breakfast and serving right through into the evening, we will offer a varied menu – all using seasonal and locally sourced ingredients.

From Easter, the Upper Deck bar will be open, offering panoramic views of HMS *Belfast* and surrounding landmarks including Tower Bridge, the Tower of London and The Shard.

The Walrus Café, situated just off the Boat Deck, is open over English school holidays and bank holiday weekends for light lunches, cakes, coffees and teas in the heart of the ship.

For group catering bookings please call **020 3116 4457**.

VOLUNTEERING

THE VOLUNTEER PROGRAMME ON HMS BELFAST HELPS TO KEEP OUR SHIP IN SHAPE

Volunteering is proving to be a growing source of support to the conservation, operation, promotion and further development of HMS *Belfast*. During our 2011–2012 year some 1,436 days were donated by volunteers in Conservation, Interaction, Office Support and our Bridge Wireless Office Radio Station.

CONSERVATION

We now have a team of more than 30 Warship Conservation Volunteers active on board who support our Conservation and Facilities Manager with the delivery of parts of the Conservation Plan for HMS *Belfast*. As a lot of the practical work involves fighting corrosion, it can be far from glamorous, but it is vital if we are jointly to keep the ship in shape for present and future visitors. Since 2007 Conservation Volunteers have worked on a variety of restoration tasks, from the ship's secondary 4-Inch armament and Bofors Guns to a Blind Fire Director Unit and Whaler.

INTERACTION AND LEARNING SUPPORT

Our Interaction Volunteers Team now offers a friendly introduction to a number of the key spaces on the visitor tour, such as the Compass Platform. Volunteers in this team offer more information on the spaces concerned to the public, and also give visitors the chance to handle authentic and replica equipment and uniforms, some of which were used when the ship was still operational.

OFFICE SUPPORT

Our volunteer programme has continued to expand, meaning we need more behind-the-scenes support. This has come from two dedicated Office Support Volunteers who attend weekly and carry out a range of duties, including helping with regular Volunteer Welcome Days to screen potential new recruits.

RADIO STATION

Royal Naval Amateur Radio Society (London Group) Volunteers have been operating radio equipment in the Bridge Wireless Office since well before our formal volunteer programme began in 2006–2007. More recently the active on board volunteer members of the group have been formally enrolled as 'Radio Section' members of the IWM volunteer team.

For more information about volunteering on board HMS *Belfast*, please visit the website, **iwm.org.uk/hmsbelfast**.

BELOW Volunteers in action